Friendly Street
NEW POETS 12

§

Steve Rood

9/3/2007

Friendly Street
NEW POETS 12

The Night is a Dying Dog • Steven Brock

Travelling • Margaret Fensom

Nectar and Light • Murray Alfredson

Friendly Street Poets

Wakefield
Press

Friendly Street Poets Incorporated
in association with
Wakefield Press
1 The Parade West
Kent Town
South Australia 5067

www.friendlystreetpoets.org.au
www.wakefieldpress.com.au

First published 2007

Cover photograph copyright © Ben Searcy
Cover design by Clinton Ellicott, Wakefield Press, and
                    Maggie Emmett, Friendly Street Poets Inc.
Typeset by Clinton Ellicott, Wakefield Press
Printed and bound by Hyde Park Press, Adelaide

ISBN 978 1 86254 741 4

Friendly Street Poets Inc. is supported by
the **South Australian Government**
through **Arts SA**.

Government
of South Australia

Arts SA

fox creek

Contents

The Night is a Dying Dog
Steven Brock
1

Travelling
Margaret Fensom
33

Nectar and Light
Murray Alfredson
61

§

the night is a dying dog

Steve Brock

Steve Brock lives in Adelaide with his wife and eight year old daughter. He has lived and travelled widely in South America, and has published his poetry and translations from the Spanish in a range of journals. In 2003 Steve completed a PhD in Australian literature at Flinders University, and he currently works as a speech writer and policy officer. He recently translated an anthology of Mapuche poets from Chile with Juan Garrido Salgado.

Acknowledgements

Some of these poems, or earlier versions of
them, have appeared in *dB Magazine*,
03 Magazine, *Gawler Bunyip*, *Hobo*,
Famous Reporter, *Sidewalk*, *Springfield Gazette*,
Malleable Jangle, *Catalyst*, *La Hoja Verde* and
the Friendly Street website.

Many thanks to Graham Rowlands for
editorial assistance in the preparation of the
manuscript; to Geoff Goodfellow for his
comments, suggestions and encouragement;
and to Juan Garrido Salgado, Richard
Hillman, Ouyang Yu, Erica Jolly and Jules
Leigh Koch for ongoing support.

To my family, Angie and Simone.

Contents

the night is a dying dog   4

lunatic   5

gabriel street   6

have you ever heard   7

in-between   8

fear   9

the city and the sea   10

autumn in adelaide   11

haiku   13

ode to a black smudge of a bird   14

unemployed   15

poem for the eight-legged imagination   16

the moon is an old woman   17

busted   18

visit from an old friend   19

juan's bilingual bicycle   20

only the sun   21

slow   22

impressions   23

coffee time   24

farewell   25

mostly water   27

birds in the refectory   28

visions on the glenelg tram   29

winter mist   31

the poem i never wrote   32

the night is a dying dog

the dawn came upon us
unexpectedly

the night, a dying dog
lay across the gutter
its black lips
offering a last quivering kiss
to the fading stars

from the taxi window
we watched the shopkeepers
take it by the tail
and drag its corpse
through the city streets

lunatic

the moon rides
my train window
as though tonight
we shall both break free
from this tiresome orbit

from these cycles
of withered leaves
and butterflies
from the dreams and rituals
of insane lovers
from the visions
of physicists and mathematicians

where are we going tonight, moon?
for this train window
is too rigid
for my visions
or your orbit

so let us take to our separate skies
you to converse with poets
of other tongues

and i to contemplate
the more palpable curves
of my lover's embrace

gabriel street

we passed by
with a greeting
of hand, mind and eye

two angels
forging paths
through the stifling afternoon

our journey as capricious
as the clouds
making love and parting
within us

we brushed shoulders
like two great skies
mouths closed to the sun

two angels
imagining beginnings and endings
and sharing a promise of the infinite

have you ever heard

have you ever heard
the opening and closing of a flower
the flight of a butterfly
or the brushed tongue of a honey eater
the setting and rising of the sun
the arrival of spring
or the first yellow step of summer
as it escapes along the parks and avenues
where we laughed and cried so much
the fall of a flower
the fall of a thousand flowers
and the precious wait of the seeds
so too i heard your love
when all was silent

in-between

i do not know
why some days we are one
and others
two people so different
that even the way
you breathe
or drink water
seems strange to me

nor why
some days we are forever
and others never again

but i do know
that in-between
i lose myself

fear

morning comes
like a fish
rising from the depths
flashing its scales
between the blinds

later you tell me
you were dreaming about fish
with monstrous faces
saying something to you underwater
you could not understand
only to scare them away

the city and the sea

i dream your hand is a shell, and raise it to my ear
we are both contained within this pearly universe
of windswept breath, in this small space
made large with longing and the will to believe
in oceans whose mouths break into the whiteness
of laughter wondering at the weight of the world
how it could be so light lying thus in the palm of your hand
pink lips smoothed with silence opening to your mind
as you close your eyes and submit to its secret sea

the imagination being the oldest of hermit crabs
making meaning of the cast off shells of this small city
usurping the anonymous skulls of passers by
indulging in the honeycombed buildings of night
or dreaming that your hand is a shell in the shape of an ear
to which my life is held, listening me into being

autumn in adelaide

it's autumn in adelaide, the river holds
a lonely gondola close to its cold heart
rippling beyond the yellow lament of plane trees
each stroke creaking and sighing for venice
or anywhere but here among the paddle boats
and their haphazard paths
this circus of colours and numbers

though still i am here, weaving a sense of place
and time in endless travels and conversation,
in memory and the half light of what could be
we go there often, caressing the edges of
a hidden world, this language of touch
and intuition where the movements of eyes
and breath are laden with meaning,
a dialogue of shapes and sounds
of colours and fragments of dream,
we let things flow and divide among themselves

it's autumn in adelaide and the shadows
of people gather long into the afternoon of
bus stops and waiting around, the poets came
and went, laughing and crying between their tents
the flamenco singers have packed up their andalusian
    lament
it's autumn in adelaide, the dancers and crowds
have returned to the folds of other lands
to a familiar movement out of here, to a pattern
of coming and going which passes me by

for it's autumn in adelaide and the skies
are thick with cloud, the cafes and pubs
are spilling their warmth onto the streets
the talk is at once high and melancholy
our destination is a tram, it will take us
to a house in holdfast bay, a journey of sudden
stops and starts, of rumblings and prolonged silences
a journey we have made our own yet do not tire
of knowing

it's autumn in adelaide and the sun makes its way gently
down our chimney, leaving a cradle of soft light
on the grate, its fingers turned upward, caught
in a gesture of abundant warmth, holding on
as though it were a memory of fire, as though
this winter may not come at all, as though we
won't have need to gather round and share its warmth
with windswept guests from other worlds

haiku

photocopier slaves
eternally close the lid
on the divine light

jimmy hendrix plays
this small city's power lines
the tempest rages

the photos and letters
metamorphosed into giant butterflies
devouring our love

i am the window
of the day
the pure dawn

storm clouds enclose
the moon in a black fist;
it slips out like yellow soap

ode to a black smudge of a bird

it was not so much a bird
as a black smudge
stuck on a bare branch of a tree
and its song was a kind of mimic
of all the car alarms
and house alarms
and early morning alarms
you've ever heard

it brought to mind
the electronic squeals
of factory workshops
the impertinent beeps
of teller machines
the honking of cars
or the spiteful cry
of schoolyard sirens

and all the other electronic paraphernalia
that tell you
you are doing something wrong
like lying in bed at 5am
praying for sleep

while that black smudge of a bird
is accompanied by a chorus of traffic
by the rise and fall
of the snoring city

unemployed

i live in the suburb of no prospects
where the streets are wide and unemployed
their gutters stiff-upper-lipped
the moon is a loafer in the day-time sky
riding vagabond clouds
only the sun is working overtime
the stifling heat coming in waves
as my dealer tells me his theory
of the history of the world
the words losing themselves
in the white noise of his living room
though i sense his argument
is much like a surfer
about to be dumped
by a centrelink breaker
finally the phone cuts in
(like a life-line)
and i run for the street
with the difficulty of a man
emerging from thunderous surf
hair and shirt wet through
a taste of salt upon my lips

poem for the eight-legged imagination

by morning
our revelations
drift through the mind
like torn webs

the eight-legged imagination
having long retreated
into the glove
of the five senses

the moon is an old woman

the moon is an old woman
peering through
venetian blinds
watching the youth on the corner
laugh and smoke

soon her head
is sticking right out
and she is even seen
to be taking a puff
as the last of the clouds
vaporise into stars;
we wait and watch the moon get high

busted

afternoon hours
come and go
with the cooing
of turtle doves

in the next room
a man waits
like an empty bottle
for evening to come

by morning his head will hang
among the geraniums
their redness brilliant
in the spring

visit from an old friend

we sit out the back
smoke and drink beer
the kitchen window
lights one side of his face
giving his eye
a reptilian hue
i wonder
why he emerged
from the rock of my past
or if i should have shed
the skin of my student days
knowing how much
my work mates
have corrupted my thought
and thinking also
it might take another 700 hundred years
for a poet to write about artificial light
as well as li po
writes about the moon

juan's bilingual bicycle

see it waiting patiently
on the steps of the state library
or protesting against pinochet
on the steps of parliament house
watch it dodge the main-stream traffic
all the way back to mile end
(handle bars raised like inverted commas)
if you are lucky
juan will invite you in
to eat empanadas
a black olive to be discovered
in each one
like the kernel of some rich poem
play chess late into the evening
converse with lorca
and neruda
in the lounge
open the doors and windows
of rooms revealed only in verse
and as he bids you farewell
on the front porch
contemplate his bilingual bicycle
leaning against the wall
the streets of adelaide translated
its spokes gleaming in the moonlight;
motion recollected in tranquillity

only the sun

he's there
sitting on the bench again
i watch him through the trees
outside my office window

late afternoon
i glance away
from my flat screen
surprised to see a blonde
sitting next to him
leaning on his shoulder

a little later
i look again
to see he is alone

it was only the sun
on the arm of his crumpled coat
huddled against his body

and when he leaves
it's only the sun

slow

I

for once i'm slow
watching a snail
close up
in the backyard
with my five year old daughter

weeks later
the snail emerges
in her drawings

II

i show my daughter
the saucepan

she cannot make out
the constellation
despite my efforts

she says
"all i see
is a big cat"

now whenever
i look up at orion
i see the cheshire cat
grinning

impressions

I

bells chime
as the workers rise
from lunch in the square

their white helmets are dusty moons
against a sea of blue shirts and pants

clutching the moonless night of my briefcase
i drift like a boat through their talk and laughter
how i miss the company of men!

II

small cultures
of smokers
gather outside buildings

and cup hands
in intimate battle
with wind and flame

III

autumn leaves
make a habit
of light

IV

reading population statistics
i leave work at five
and find myself
another of brack's pencils
attracting and repelling
in the ebb and flow of traffic

coffee time

my colleague tells me about a seminar
he is working on
while i remind him
the average person
fears public speaking more than death

i ask him what the paper is about
and he says
it's about the coming of christ
and what our lives would be like afterwards

just as i ask him to elaborate
someone else walks into the room
and the conversation shifts
to public transport and the weather

i sip my coffee
still thinking about life under the new administration

no doubt
there'd be another review
he would come
with his own advisers

maybe my colleague
would receive
special consideration
as a true believer

but i have a feeling
i'd still be taking that call
at 10am
five days of the week

coffee time?

farewell

every now and then
we gather in the staff room
and eat cake
for another farewell

before the boss
opens his mouth
i know he'll let her down

we eat our cake
applaud
pass around
the over-sized card

at lunch
i walk around town
my face so dour
nobody asks me for change

the street performers
let me pass unnoticed

and i recognise
the usual bums

one guy i've seen
pushing the same trolley
and boxes
for over a decade

i saw him once
in a second hand book-store
with a book
on military history

looking at him right now
makes me reassess
my own strategy

whether the worry
about academic titles
and career progression
has really paid off

and if i'll have icing
on my cake

mostly water

elbows resting
on the front gate
i lean into
my noisy street
and train the binoculars
on the craters
visible just before
the 3/4 moon folds over
into darkness

some people are like this
exposed
without any atmosphere
to absorb
incoming objects
and those other impacts
disguised so well

we live in the zone
oblivious
to cause
but not always effect

otherwise
we are mostly water

birds in the refectory

the sparrow and i
devour the crumbling gifts
left on the saucers and side plates
of the perpetual present

hopping from table to table
whistling
'it's a living'
beneath the fallen sky

weighed down
by forgotten wings

visions on the glenelg tram

i saw robert dessaix
on the 1929 glenelg tram
escaping the writers week crowd
he sat alone and unknown

i read moby dick
until the curved wooden ceiling
resembled neruda's residence at isla negra
built like a boat for the unmoving captain

forgetting my melville one morning
i was lost at sea amidst the creak of timber

i read don quixote
and the passing trams
were gallant knights engaged in battle
but my work was done

and the driver
framed in the light of the cabin window
reminds me each evening
of van gogh's postman
only clean shaven

and i did see patrick white
on the priority seats for the aged

and as for proust
his long sentences need rails

and neale hunter
we read aloud your introduction
to *shanghai journal*
and it was as though you'd never died

winter mist

windows become
a second skin

sensitive to touch
and breath alike

diffusing the light
of a speeding world

until the universe is reduced
to a voice on the radio

contained within the dim
green horizon of the dash

leaving us with football scores
and a haptic writing

the poem i never wrote

the other day
i thought out a poem
and never wrote it down
or i wrote it
and lost it anyway
or more likely
wrote the poem
and found that it was no good
the idea was a broken umbrella
not even an inside out umbrella
but one that never opened in the first place
despite having carried it around all day

Travelling

Margaret Fensom

Margaret Fensom arrived in Adelaide from London by steamship in 1947 at the age of four, and has lived here ever since. She is widowed and has two adult daughters and three grandchildren. She completed a BA and, many years later, an MA in Creative Writing at the University of Adelaide.

Margaret lives in a cottage in Norwood. Her interests include public transport, solar and wind energy, the environment and social justice. She enjoys travelling by train, and has travelled by rail through the UK and Europe, and across Russia by Trans Siberian Railway.

Acknowledgements

Some of these poems have appeared in the
Friendly Street readers, *Staples, Multicultural
Life*; in the anthologies *The Starving Writers'
Guide to Absolutely Everything, Iron Lace*
and *'Traveling'* and on the websites of
Friendly Street Poets and Kensington and
Norwood Writers Group.

To Leslie, Tess, Maureen, Helen and Ursula
for their friendship in writing; Dawn Colsey;
poets at Kensington and Norwood Writers,
A Passion of Poets and Friendly Street; and to
my father, who first encouraged me in
my poetry.

Contents

Almonds 36

Night Imaginings 37

Travel Journal 38

Venice 39

Wind Power 40

Framboises 41

Czech Republic 43

Vladivostok 45

Leaving Vladivostok 46

Metro 47

Bridges 48

Home Coming 49

Paranoia 50

Liberation 51

Reflections 52

December 53

Spider Rope 54

Spider Lace 55

Hot Rods and Tulle 56

Thirty First of December 57

Almond Moon 58

Afterwards 59

Fireworks 60

Almonds

Almonds bloom
like moths flying in the night
almost white as hail
lying like icy flowers
upon the ground.

Silver soft as moths' wings
and the grey green grass
that grows on windswept dunes
the bitter jelly almonds are encased
in furry pods

waiting, waiting
for birds with rainbow feathers
apple green backs and scarlet berry throats
to eat them in the nick of time.

We gather broken shells.

Night Imaginings

What is that?
What dreadful phantom grows out of night
feeding on grief?

It is the white rose seen
dimly against dark tree.
It is the hidden wallflower
of lilac hue.
It is the spider running in the grass
under dark dew.

Travel Journal

I have found birds
hiding among irises
the pale orange lilies
and blue leaves
of my journal

which hides arum lilies
white irises by river
stone bridges over the Seine
dreaming afternoons in boats
pale lochs with mountain shadows
and the turquoise sea of Venice.

But how much stranger
beyond my imagination
are the flowers which I have never seen
birds hiding in dreams.

Venice

Venice is pale
like shallow water stretched under sunrise
turquoise mirror lagoon where boats move
among cypress islands with their old stone walls
rainbow stucco and lace doilies,
domed churches under hazy sky
arched windows where no-one looks
over the dim canal
pale pastel flakes that break and dissolve
into the bitter sea.

Wind Power

Once I saw a butterfly
in a wheatfield
in Denmark
white windmills across a little lake
with daisy petal sails
garnering the wind.

But when I returned
they were grey and small
shadows of electricity
upon the landscape.

Framboises

Framboises, rich red raspberries
ten francs a punnet

and I who have battled
the SNCF
also the Irish ferry company
whose people only speak French
trying to book a passage to Ireland
I love this city, Paris, but must leave

climb the long stairs from the Metro
past birch forest mural with pink flowers
faint fringe of spring,
walk past open shop fronts
see them
rich red raspberries.
How can I resist?

In my room on the sixth floor
no lift
I eat them all,
gaze from my balcony in the roof
at the white apartments opposite
pale shutters and geranium window boxes
blooms on the balcony.

One apartment is *à vendre*.

Had I but wealth enough and time.

Somehow I feel at home in these streets
where people speak another language,
but for me
no fine French cooking could compare
with tart sweet ruby red fresh raspberries.

Czech Republic

The dark blue engine
white banded, buttercup striped
stands among the daisies
that grow between rail lines.

Train passes
windows square
windows seen in windows
trains beyond trains.

Green domed building
wilted flowers
faded mosaics
broken glass.

White marble pillars
pulpit of gold
sweet voice of student
singing in great church.

Art students by the river
making faces at me.
It's not them I'm snapping.
Tram over bridge.

It's humming, dancing
over the wide grey river
for lands of birch and spruce
mosaics by the station
dusty windows
faded flowers on platform
copper domes turned green
and white swans on a dark river.

Vladivostok

I'm getting to know the old city
bursting at its seams with cars
in narrow streets
the paint peeled wood
tin gable roofs
elegant old buildings and concrete block flats
trees with honeysuckle flowers
high heeled blondes walking treacherous footpaths
ships on the grey harbour
green parks
and the huge bronze statue
of the tiger
perhaps still lurking
in some far forest.

Leaving Vladivostok

Music plays.
Imperceptibly
the train begins to move
past high rise flats, factories and rusted iron
pale midsummer sea
people and goats
green oaks
allotments by small houses made of wood
and on and on for three white nights
three days of meadows and birches
cities with strange names
wide and narrow rivers
huts below hills, cows and potato patches.
We go with other travellers
children, mothers, soldiers, train drivers
the same great journey for them
and us, the strangers, discovering their land.

Metro

Underground we visit strange places

Yellow flowers in Amsterdam
bright bunches for sale in a grey tunnel.

Roman artefacts in deep cave
where Stockholm Tunnelbana travel
to blocks of flats in pine forests
signposts to *bibliotek* and *Folkpark*.

In Paris you need only see what you want to see
and if you get lost
there will always be a station nearby
to take you somewhere you've heard of before.

Easier to get lost underground in London
where you need to know
north south
clockwise anti-clockwise
than in Paris where the destination sign
tells you where you are heading
large and dark blue
on a blue and white notice
on white tiles
and the murals
O the murals
at the *gare Abbesses*
birch trees and snow
and the faint blush
of spring approaching.

Bridges

Bridges cross from one place to another:
Right Bank to Left Bank of the Seine
over a low arched bridge of stone;
over the green canal at Annecy
that flows out of the mountain-rimmed lake
past bridges with flower baskets by canals,
old buildings with their feet in water;
Bridge of Sighs and many other bridges
over canals where gondolas glide
and pink stucco houses flake away
as the sea rises;
bridge of latticed steel over the harbour
in Sydney where the hills come down
to the blue water
and somewhere remembered
are echoes of Bennelong and the dispossessed
submarines sharks and yacht races
white and coloured sails
billowing over the riffled water.

But there was no bridge
over the Jordan in the days of Joshua,
whether the city of Jericho stood or not,
so between here and what is to come
there is no bridge but that which faith constructs.

Home Coming

I see the sparkle of your imminent arrival
car headlights broken by the pebbled glass.
And I wait
remembering my own youth
for the soft scratching sound of a key
thud of the wood framed door
and footsteps in the hall.

Paranoia

My house is full of invisible people
biro burglars and sink stopper thieves
the people who put papers at the bottom of piles
the moment they touch the table
one-footed sock snitchers and shoe shufflers

objects that practice domestic camouflage
queues of important documents
waiting to be found
at least six months after they are needed.

If only my guardian angel were a filing clerk . . .

Liberation

Every morning
year upon year
I washed the dishes

till one day
the dishes turned to leaves
and I fed them to my goat.

Reflections

In a courtyard pool
light gives infinite depth
where slate dips
countering the thrust
of the old vine.

Lavender flowers
seek earth's centre.
A fan palm reaches downwards
and a rose petal
lies beached on mossy shore.

Far below
under vine trellis
is the sky.

December

In dry gardens
agapanthus buds
their green stalks
like swans' necks
open white umbels
and mist blue flower heads
surprising summer.

White flowered bushes
perfume the dusk.
The dark blue sky
of nine o'clock
is pale around the edges
as the orange crescent moon
seems to grow towards its setting
holding the ghost moon in its arms.

Spider Rope

Dust falls from broken cobweb.
I snap a spider rope.

Summer broken
crickets sing
under the dreaming goldenrod.

Spider Lace

She hangs her silken threads upon
rose thorns which are the points of her verandah.

And never does the sun stop at her walls
or the rain beat in vain upon her windows.

Hot Rods and Tulle

Orange cars with white ribbons
belch smoke
fogging the road with their roars.

Bell towers
hazy in mist.

Powdered bridesmaids
in lilac
carry stiff bouquets.

All the coloured wrappings
of love and hope
twist in cold winds.

Thirty First of December

It is the last evening.

Flame tree flowers
yellow-green cypress
darkening sky.

Frothy cream blossoms
on street trees.

The sun has that golden honey stain
as it drains away.

Green leaves fall into shadow

Will tomorrow come?

Almond Moon

Mild pearl, our tide rock
floats in a clear pale sky.
Blossoms blow like ash.

Afterwards

Once the sun shone
on the walls of my house
flowers bloomed in my garden
birds sang in the trees
and I was friendly with my neighbours.

Now I see
rocks and rubble
and the midnight glove of fear
strokes me with its fingers.

Fireworks

Sydney Harbour: Midnight,
New Year's Eve 2002

The Chinese invented gunpowder
and made firecrackers.

Would that humankind
had thought of no worse use
than these peace lilies
flaring their petals
over the dark harbour.

Nectar and Light

Murray Alfredson

Murray Alfredson is a retired librarian and lecturer, and a former Buddhist Associate to the Multi-faith Chaplaincy at Flinders University. He graduated in German and History from the University of Melbourne and holds a research masters degree from the University of Wales. He began to write poetry in his undergraduate days and resumed in retirement. He has published poems and essays on Buddhism, spirituality and inter-faith matters in journals in Australia and the UK.

Acknowledgements

Some poems in this collection have been
published in *Cadenza, Eremos* and *Overland.*

I thank my best friend and sharpest critic,
my wife, Jyoti, whose support has got me
writing again and helped me to stay with it.
I dedicate this collection to her. Her love is
large and resilient.

I should also like to thank Graeme Webster
for his good humoured teaching.

Contents

To Jyoti, the flame I   64

To Jyoti, the flame II   65

An Jyoti, die Flamme   66

Gossamer   67

I think, therefore ...?   68

Ch'an music II   70

The round   71

To Wolfgang Magg   72

Mason's garden   73

From: Birds and other *dukkha*   74

Nectar   75

Midnight music   76

In memoriam gemini mei   77

'... with birth as condition, ...'   82

Requiem   83

The pipes in minor key ...   84

Pectoral   85

Sacred space   86

Sunsets I and II   87

Night piece   88

To Jyoti, the flame I*

Unsteady flame and mutable
  that wavers in each breeze
and flickers with each rise and fall
  of heat and gases,

why, o why, I cry, who yearn
  to rest in constancy,
must you always judder when
  I need you steady?

as one who craves a glowing gold,
  a light that ever lingers,
as one who arrogates to hold
  your holy flame with fingers.

*Jyoti (Sanskrit): light, flame

To Jyoti, the flame II

I think of you as now my sun begins to set;
if only I could fly to you!
The cloud glows underneath and swells out like a sail;
home I feel myself now driven,
glad by you to lie.
And when, beloved bliss, beyond one breathless night
my new sun drives away the early grey with gold,
o may I love you still throughout the life to come!

An Jyoti, die Flamme

Ich denke dein, als mir die Sonne untergeht;
o könnte ich nur zu dir fliegen!
Die Wolke unten glüht und wie ein Segel bläht;
nach Hause fühl ich mich getrieben,
froh bei dir zu liegen.
Und wenn nach atemsloser Nacht, beliebte Wonne,
vertreibt mit Gold das Frühgrau mir die neue Sonne;
o möge ich dich noch durchs nächste Leben lieben!

ihres 50sten Geburtstags zur Feier

Gossamer

Love is but
a fragile thing,
a dew-decked thread,
a gossamer
of thought and feelings
spun in space
between two beings.

There is no anchor,
no saying, Love me
for love's sake only.
Naught holds securely.
That fragile silk
is all there is,
and dewdrops
all its sparkle.

Let then those
who choose love's way
lightly tread
and learn to be
moment by moment
skilful tenders
of gossamer,
delaying a while,
a little while,
the pain of parting.

I think, therefore …?

Like grass on dunes we cling.
No, we are the dunes;
with flimsy crust,
with grass and scrub,
we hope to hold
against the dry,
the drift from shifting winds.

But there is naught
to us but change,
loose heaps
of happenings.

Reds, greens, tree-shapes,
harmonies and blares,
stench and fragrance,
tastes and touches
prod us.

These feel fair
or foul
or just so so.

The inner eye
twigs or not.

Ideas and wants
walk through or linger;
the treading crumbles
fragile dune-crust.

All registers
a while,
then fades.

How is it then,
we say: we are?

Bodies age;
senses dull;
thoughts flitter;
feelings shift
like windblown sand;
and consciousness
candle like
flickers and dies.

There is no anchor
nothing holds;
dry sands tumble.
Dying blades and haulms,
they sway, they tremble.

Ch'an music II*

Drink in a while
the image of
an unfilled teacup.

Enter that space
flawless, open,
enclosed by porcelain walls.

Sit still, sit quietly:
just breathe and wait;
cherish no thought.

Then, perhaps, in silence
beyond the stillness
you will find the void.

Dwell inside that space,
dwell but do not fill it;
do not seek to grasp it.

For there is neither hold
nor holding. Let go.
Be still and know

the void as void.
Hear that soundless singing.

*Ch'an (Chinese): from dhyâna (Sanskrit)
 the meditative absorptions (=Zen)

The round

Aeons are vast
so vast indeed
– the Buddha said –
a granite mountain
leagues high, leagues wide,
lightly brushed
by floating silk
one stroke each hundred years,
would sooner wear away.

Past collapse
and birth of countless
worlds and stars,
past births and deaths
of galaxies –
countless aeons
long we tumble
through *saṃsarâ*

To Wolfgang Magg*

You slump behind your cello;
trousers swallow sunken chest;
head supports a meagre crop
long faded into white.

Fragile moments you create:
fingers tremble; bow-arm shakes;
still with mastery you coax
strings and shaven wood

to sing with mellow voice and firm
a song to match your inner harmonies –
each note and bar a triumph
over all your eighty years.

*The brother-in-law of a late friend who
 translated poems of Christian Morgenstern

Mason's garden

Impeccable
in placement
and in shaping,
row on row
of topiary
in greys and reds.

Slim, polished,
felspar flecked
those granite leaves:
crystals tight-locked
long in durance
they patient stand.

Unwritten leaves
for lives waiting
final transplant.

From: Birds and other *dukkha*

Raven, wind ruffled
velvet waistcoat: the gutter
now your charnel ground.

This loving service:
piece by piece he feeds his friend
to sky burial.

Hand strikes frozen air –
night long through skull's hollow, glass
gong reverberates.

Snake, red-bellied black,
hisses, swings; man inches back;
silence glides downhill.

Slender trace of ants –
monk in orange robes seeks new
meditation path.

Light glints from pinhead
eyes; finger furrows mouse-fur
despite autumn plague.

Nectar

Mint-bush flecked with flowers of magenta;
I pluck them from their calyx and
savour that tiny tang of nectar.
Likewise I nip and drain sharp
hood-juice from nasturtiums.
Two little pleasures these, too short,
too quick to form attachments –
a prick of piquance; gone.

Ponder, though, the bee, who takes
her nectar without ripping, nipping
and fills thereby the flower's purpose:
by far the bee's my better.

Midnight music

Say not that midnight is the witching hour
as though midwinter midnight boded ill;
graveyards do not yawn here; nor does hell
breathe forth contagion. Here magpies float
their break-voiced fluting through the frosted air;
gonad-swollen, juice-charged before indeed
the rising sap bursts wattles into flower,
those urgent singers fill the nights with call-notes,
prey now to the magic of the Mother.

In memoriam gemini mei

I

Those we love have greatest power to wound;
and brother you have hurt me sorely.
Not yet old, you had no need to die.
Monozygotes live so interwoven,
even half a continent apart;
skeins of thought thread in and out.
They hung between us in the air
as once hung cords of blood in amniotic dim –
two minds, two hearts with shared placenta
gazing through one dull red spidered light.
Left lung you've torn from me, ripped half my chest.

II

You came to me, my brother, in the night.
You saw shock fell me, my life-will bleeding fast.
You closed my gaping chest; you staunched my wounds.
I woke to find your cautery had soothed.
Yet still I yearned to join with you and friends,
both long and recent dead, in golden light,
to share again the pleasures of like minds.
My death wish lifts a little, though my sight
is blurred with tears that well on to my cheek.
Slow, so slow, the sharpness dulls to ache.

III

You lie before me yet it is not you,
hands clasped, close coffined, lips, as often, tucked
at corners to a smile; a faint death odour
lifts past oils from your mottled skin.

Your head, your brow, are cold to lips and fingers.
And yet it is not you. The strings that tied
the bundles of your being hang cut and loose;
form only stays, a focus for our tears,
for words of celebration and farewell
as we commit your remnants to the flames.

IV

Was it so great, surprise to learn that death
cuts loose, but does not end all thought and sense?
to see, but not with eyes grown heavy, frantic
measures to revive? to hear the cries?
to see but not to feel the pumping hands?
to know the body was beyond repair?
to know too high the cost to repossess?
to stay apart and leave us with the lesser grief?
Ever sceptical you lived; you counted
nothing beyond the floating ties and bundles.
Surprise to find you still had tasks?
surprise to walk still? surprise to fly?
and burdensome to mend the love-wounds left?
to find a path to speak? untangling strings
of hurt you left behind? You did this, brother,
even though new fingers were not firm.
Your words you could not use, but only speak
through others' minds and words, blunt instruments.
Strangely you spoke through poets past, through Goethe,
Heine, Kürenberg, and used their words,
their flights, as vehicles for your challenges.
Such style! Now dead and living march together.

V

Slowly, slowly you withdraw, your voice,
no voice, which strokes the strings of mind, grows quiet;
your business with the living soon will close,
old hurts resolved, no cankers left to fester,
all residues for us to bear and heal,
not you. You have worked hard and skilfully
since searing lungs and drowning in your acid.
Move forward; almost done your tasks with us;
but as you edge away, a second time
I feel cold round my throat and warm in eyes
now subtly rising waters of bereavement.

VI

Almost I envy you, my brother, moving
on to challenges I do not know.
Beside the faintest teasing glimpses, vapours
merely, we nothing see of the beyond;
we sometimes dread that huge unknown, a gaping
emptiness, a chasm shadowed by
death's open lips. And yet no dread I feel,
an envy rather of my twin who marches
into schools I do not know, while I must wait,
my twin unhampered by a wool-wad head,
with mind not tied to heaviness and migraine.
A greed I feel to know the cosmos you
are learning; yes, to fly with mind less fettered;
a greed, no less, yet here with head and back ache
is my world, with white-haired darling, with sister,
grown-up children, nephews, children's children.
I slowly set aside my greed, a book worn out;

beside scarred emptiness within my chest
I stack the things of now, the loves of now,
take up my tasks and wait and care.

VII

Within a womb a foetus forms and grows,
a restless imp who swims the tiny chamber;
Caius, Caia – that we do not know –
your first grandchild you never knew would be.
I view those flecked sound-pictures; a restful care
has kindled in my chest, filled lung and heart,
grasped rib and muscle, a nurture for the forming
head and brain, hands, fingers, feet, that not
yet infant who must move months off and be
expelled into the greater world, then swaddled
snug against the shock of air and space.
O mountain-like the task ahead, to grow
to meet the fearsome vastness! At times it lurks
in sleep, beyond the veil of eyelids, at times
in daylight glare as from a peak where ridge
by ridge the eye is led into the greying
distance. And subtle, watchful is your parents'
task; a little I stand back as though
grandfather to that dawning life, a role,
my brother, you are no longer here to play.

VIII

It does not dazzle; does not glare. The indoor
daylight flicks, it seems, just faintly brighter,
almost beneath discernment. I see no cause
for that. I see no clearer. The flimsy clouds
still veil the sun, still scatter as before,

as ever, the southern light back through the window,
a soft suffusion. Slowly eyes and brain
accommodate, and yet that subtle lightness
lingers, a mood almost and not a lumen.
I sense your presence in the room, I sense
you here beside me, sense your touch on arm
and ribs, a touch, no touch, an almost touch,
influx, a warm infusion rather, through
my quiet parts and brain. We know your presence,
know that you are with us all our days.

'… with birth as condition, …'

for Natasha, 1974–2005

Before our birth we carry death within us,
from the first moment of the male which burrows
through the ovum wall, from the faint flicker

in fallopian dark, each moment lived
now moves us closer to our last, be that
before implanting or ninety years beyond.

But in a special way that hung between
those coupling gametes, your death lay hid to form
a tiny spot; that berry swelled and ripened.

Silently it lurked inside your skull
until it blistered, burst and bled – a flash,
a headache came. You slept and slipped away.

Requiem

for Natasha, 1974–2005

A long transparent tunnel stretches up
far, far to light that glints and glows along it;
from far away we see her climb toward
the glow; her hair wafts out behind
as in a breeze. With trembling touch our thoughts
are peopled round her as she treads the path
of purple to the awesome that she does not know,
nor we, the all-at-once sharp light that pierces
through our inmost being and leaves no shadow.

Her name means birth. And she has born two girls
and pushed them to the glare of this life. O may
this birth that she is taking better be
for her than here, and may our thoughts that float
behind and hairlike stroke her face, o may
they strengthen her ahead in her unknown.

The pipes in minor key …

The pipes in minor key, they haunt the air
and resonate within the lungs and heart.
Tears overflow down cheeks as hand by hand
on tapes the shoe-box coffin's lowered in
that little grave. The sun still shines, though wind
is bleak to match the mood. And thus it is
we let fall our clods of loam, an earth
to earth committal, and hug in sorrow shared.

An hour before it was, with shock it dawned:
that tiny china doll, that figure dressed
in bridal white (or was it christening?)
had been a human child, thrust forth too soon
from womb to light and air, from warm to cold.
Two hours she'd lingered on her mother's chest.
In love begotten, born and died, interred
to lie within the bosom of the Mother.

Pectoral

(variation on Paul Celan)

No mere tattoo
will do for your name
once darling.

Letter by letter,
crisp *sans serif,*
of brass you're inserted
and sutured
under the skin
of my chest.

There you lie
nestled in acid
adipose.

Lifelong you'll stay,
and beyond,
above my heart
to verdigris
the fat, the
blood, the
skin.

Sacred space

'Come in and see our mosque!' the students beamed,
shook bare their feet, and ushered me inside.
The walls of concrete blocks were unadorned;
a simple trough for feet and head and hands;
some mats were heaped against one wall, and strewn
towards the north-west corner that served as *qibla*.

And when it happened, Jesus was not hurt,
nor yet his Dad, and neither their beloved
Muhammad. For such are slow to anger; but sad
they were, and heavy hearted for their friends.

The odour bit them hard, those lads; it struck
them in the face. They stared in disbelief;
for in those empty hours between the prayer times
someone dropped upon the floor, centred
in that sacred space, a human turd.

Sunsets

(variations on a theme of Hölderlin)

I

A god salutes us: flinging his molten gold
    across the city sky, the Sustainer takes
        his leave. But no one lifts his eyes, nor
            heeds as that pledge to return now filters

like powdered fire silently through the noise
    and rush of Melbourne's traffic – except some youth,
        perhaps, who slides a train door open,
            inwardly stirred to an ancient worship.

II

The sun is set; the cloudscape once softly drawn
    in gold and rust now fades to a single grey.
        All glow has gone. The wind bites coldly.
            Bear with your sorrow: the dawn comes slowly.

Night piece

The owls rebuked me. Silent as stars they came
   on still wings, lit wings, bellies agleam from street-
      and park-lamps; stars they were, those strong, those
         silently ongliding points of brightness.

They took them forms of birds in approaching, fleet
   and silent birds commanding the shadowed park;
      that silence, rippling rush of silence,
         called on the sensitive ear to hark them.

The stars are gods, they tell us of old, so far,
   so vast they cannot know that we men have hearts.
      From sea, from mountaintop we see them,
         moon set or hidden, and all else blackness.

They thrust long spears through ages of empty dark,
   sharp points of light that tremor against our eye;
      and steeled restraint of vibrant shoulders
         coldly compels us to kneel and worship.

But who would dream to gaze from the noise of streets,
   the blaze of lamp and neon, toward the sky?
      We've pitched a tent of glare above us,
         shielding ourselves from those night-honed lances.

Yet still the high gods come, in a kinder form:
   they slip beneath our dome of defence as hawks
      of night and haunt the air around us,
         patiently calling our eye and wonder.

How many, many nights have you flown above
and I not seen you, gods in the flesh? How long
had you to wait before my heart's door?
Brain was so buzzing, I failed to hear you.

Friendly Street New Poets Series

Friendly Street New Poets 1 (1995)
The wolf stares in • Geoff Kemp
Silver from Black • Yve Louis
Suburban Bonsai • John Malone

Friendly Street New Poets 2 (1996)
Picking up the Pieces • Anna Brooks
Life in the Oort Cloud • Jenny Weight
Scarves of Sand • David Cookson

Friendly Street New Poets 3 (1997)
The Red Shoes • Louise Nicholas
Her Mother's Arms • Stephen Lawrence
Mending the Dingo Fence • Richard Hillman

Friendly Street New Poets 4 (1998)
The Right Side of My Face • Junice Direen
A Strip of Negatives • Jules Leigh Koch
Boy Stunner • Jason Sweeney

Friendly Street New Poets 5 (1999)
I Say . . . • Ioana Petrescu
Twisting the Rainbow • Maureen Vale
The Love Within My Stare • Julian A. Zytnik

Friendly Street New Poets 6 (2000)
Rain Falls on the Garden • John De Laine
Fish Star Glinting • Alison Manthorpe
maiden voyage • Ray R. Tyndale

Friendly Street New Poets 7 (2002)
Travelling with Bligh • Kate Deller-Evans
Night Fishing • Jim Puckridge
Triangular Light • Melanie Duckworth

Friendly Street New Poets 8 (2003)
The Windmill's Song • Elaine Barker
Kite Lady • Tess Driver
Fine Rain Straight Down • David Mortimer

Friendly Street New Poets 9 (2004)
Peeling Onions • Jill Gloyne
Crescent Moon Caught Me • Judith Ahmed
Scoffing Gnocchi • Linda Uphill

Friendly Street New Poets 10 (2005)
Stealing • Libby Angel
Deaf Elegies (from Virginia Woolf's Record Store) • Robert J. Bloomfield
Sparrow in an Airport • rob walker

Friendly Street New Poets 11 (2005)
low background noise • Cameron Fuller
words free • Simone G Matthews
jars of artefacts • Rachel Manning